My Student Pledge Journal

Samson Yung-Abu

To order additional copies of this book, contact:
Xlibris
0800-056-3182
www.xlibrispublishing.co.uk
Orders@ Xlibrispublishing.co.uk

CONTENTS

My Student Pledge Journal

GEEK COMMUNITY
LEARNING THROUGH STUDENTS

"The power of the world is really contained in knowing the unknown, the unfamiliar, and the unaccustomed, all of which are available to us through education."

—Samson Y. A.

_____

_____

_____

_____

_____

_____

My Student Pledge Journal

STUDENT'S PROFILE

GEEK COMMUNITY
LEARNING THROUGH STUDENTS

- Name: _____
- Age: _____
- Personality: _____
- School: _____
- Academic year: _____
- Kind of learner (visual, auditory, kinaesthetic): _____
- Hobby: _____
- Talent: _____
- Motivation: _____
- Career wish: _____
- Mentor: _____
- Best friend: _____
- Worst friend: _____
- Best teacher: _____
- Worst teacher: _____
- Favourite food: _____
- Crush: _____
- Favourite celebrity: _____

My Student Pledge Journal

STUDENT'S PLEDGES

GEEK COMMUNITY
LEARNING THROUGH STUDENTS

- I pledge to be committed.
- I pledge to improve myself.
- I pledge to be motivated.
- I pledge to stand out.
- I pledge to be outstanding.
- I pledge to make my parents proud.
- I pledge to be inspired and to inspire others to inspire themselves and others.
- I pledge to take actions rather than procrastinate.
- I pledge to enforce discipline in my education.
- I pledge to give education a new meaning and purpose and to add to existing techniques to help my educational institute become better, safer, and prouder of its community.

My Student Pledge Journal

INTRODUCTION

Personally, I feel that the first stage to performing well academically is to remind yourself that you are a student and that education is of paramount importance in attaining your full academic potential. It might sound clichéd, but there is no denying the fact that you need to absolutely commit to and earnestly desire to seriously engage with your academics in order to realise your full potential as a student. To make excellence the norm and not the exception, you must realise that your future is inevitably predicated on what you have the ability to do with your present, signified by your academic responsibilities. This is because the ultimate decision to do better and become well equipped to enhance your current and future academic performance depends on just one person, and that is you.

Some students go through the education process with a distinct sense of detachment, as opposed to proactive engagement. They feel their curriculum is overloaded with lifeless learning content that amplifies their stress levels, confusion, and seclusion. They also tend to experience a sensory overload and feel as if they are drowning in a seemingly endless ocean of misery. At times, they do not feel engaged with the learning process anymore because they do not think that they have what it takes, or that they have any control over the outcome of their grades. As a result, they begin to feel frustrated and out of place.

As a postgraduate student, I have learned a number of lessons, and one valuable takeaway I will gladly share is the art of keeping a journal that tracks your journey of becoming a better student. Have you ever thought about giving up everything related to academics because everything seems out of place and far-fetched and the whole educational system seems messed up, cluttered, ambiguous, and unsatisfying? That used to be my story year after year *until* I decided I wanted to improve and make things much more cinched. The only thing that truly helped me do this was getting organised! It improved my grades, which I wanted, but I also got more than I had bargained for. My mind-set also improved when I began to function in an organised manner and write down everything in a journal at the end of each week. This included the good stuff, the bad stuff, and even the worst of the worst. I wrote down everything I felt strongly about, and I reflected deeply on it whilst seeking ways to decipher what worked, what didn't work, why it all worked, or why nothing worked at all.

Previously, I was never as passionate about education as I have been over the past two years; now, I absolutely love the very thought of learning new material and acquiring new information. Until two years back, I erroneously thought that top-grade students are a special breed and have an extra edge, and some students just cannot compete with them. However, this state of mind is extremely dangerous because it shrinks our sense of self-worth and keeps us from attaining what we can actually attain. It is, therefore, imperative that we believe in the concept of *equalised academic possibilities*— that we are no exception to academic success. Becoming a better student isn't as difficult as it sounds—nowhere near it. I have had all the grades possible, ranging from A+ to U, but it was all a learning curve. I am happy I got them all, but most important, I am proud that I overcame them all. Now, I can safely say that I have made significant progress and become a worthy contributor to the student community.

I created this pledge journal to give you the opportunity to reorganise your academics and your educational life at large in a way that makes sense to you, not just for today but for every single day. This includes making your tomorrow better than yesterday. By implementing the tips mentioned in this journal, you will be able to identify your best way of studying, remember things better, stay focused with progressive clarity and consistency, and inevitably initiate a productive way to engage with your curriculum.

My Student Pledge Journal

A STUDENT'S PURPOSE FOR KEEPING A JOURNAL

It is paramount that we seek ways and opportunities to become effective students so that we know how to identify strengths and weaknesses, organise them in a manner so we know where to find them, analyse them, and take practical measures to improve on them. Against this backdrop, a journal is instrumental in the collection and collation of relevant ideas and information.

After engaging with reading materials—books, magazines, online research, or anything that stands out—I make it a point to note the materials' key facts in my student journal. The habit of maintaining a journal makes a student subjectively better at attaining his or her objective goals. It helps students assemble scattered pieces of information in a way that makes sense, is concise and consistent, and remains easily accessible. When a student takes relevant notes, the notes tend to make a lot of sense when he or she comes back to them in a week's time. In fact, this habit induces succour and makes an uncomfortable week rather comfortable. It also allows a student to manage his or her educational affairs, highlight current academic competence, and nurture creativity and improvement in a seamless manner. Equally, keeping a journal helps students stay cognisant of the fact that their yesterday matters today for a better tomorrow. Put simply, *if* they choose to analyse their yesterdays today, it will empower them to find ways to improve the prospects of their tomorrows.

Analogously, a journal streamlines the consolidation of a week's worth of activities in a way that helps students better manage their time, thoughts, and progress. As a case in point, your student pledge journal will help you reflect on what is most important to you by the end of the week. Keeping a student pledge journal gives a definite direction to your desire to learn and take the much-needed initiative in setting a relevant schedule and engaging with your academic material in its entirety. It enables you to chronicle key concepts and ideas that you are not particularly familiar with so that you can come back to them later and find their true essence.

My Student Pledge Journal

TIPS FOR REACHING YOUR FULL ACADEMIC POTENTIAL

GEEK COMMUNITY
LEARNING THROUGH STUDENTS

Acknowledge personal responsibility.

While goals remain subjective to students, we generally wish to attain better grades; impress our teachers and tutors; meet deadlines; have an all-powerful brain with a heightened ability to recall facts and concepts; achieve more with less effort; make our parents proud; outsmart our classmates and friends; and have less stress during our studies, our presentations, our exams, and our life in general.

Are these wishes attainable? The answer is a resounding *yes*! However, this answer is also highly predicated on how we organise our academic affairs and how dedicated we stay to daily synchronising all our aspirations in a way that promotes individuality and creativity. Personally speaking, having a dedicated pledge journal has helped me tremendously in managing my academic commitments, and it has enabled me to engage meaningfully with my studies. When it comes to academic achievements, not just who you are matters. Everything you can do to become what you want to be matters too! That became my unflinching motto, and it helped me stay focused and cinched.

While it is impossible for students to retain information like Wikipedia can, everyone does have the ability to learn more and maximise his or her academic potential. For some, it seems to come more naturally than it does for others; however, academic success can be attained by anyone who appreciates the essence of education, acknowledges his or her ability to learn new information, and takes practical steps on a daily basis to become a better student.

In essence, this implies that, given the right level of personal contribution in terms of how we structure our learning, we can have a greater amount of autonomy over our academic goals and how we overcome academic barriers. I concede that learning is subjective and pattern dependent; however, keeping a student journal helps you maintain the efficacy of learning by regulating your strengths and weaknesses whilst making your progress more visual and accessible. Using a journal in such a disciplined manner helped me invest my time better, gave me a platform to analyse my progress, and in effect enabled me to make more discerning choices in my exciting journey of attaining my full academic potential for the year.

Appreciate the role of education.

Education gets challenging and intimidating at times, but that needs to be the case if we want to improve and progress to a level that showcases excellence in academic performance. However, it is comforting to know that education is not about creating a myopic shortfall; it is designed to give us wings to fly and reach places we've only dreamt of. Furthermore, it is important that we have awareness of the required level of engagement and commitment to bring into our academic lives as students to shape a better future. Very rarely does anyone tell us how valuable it is to be a committed, ambitious, and efficiently educated student. No one tells us the how and why we really need to seek improvement techniques to attain our academic potential every year. I would not have been able to write this book if I lacked this gratitude towards education. It is therefore logical to surmise that having a penchant for putting words together does not suffice when it comes to going above and beyond in establishing novel ideas and creating a platform where others can lay their foundations for moving forward.

Some of the most famous people in the world have one thing in common: their devotion to education. Thus, education is a worldwide phenomenon with far-reaching implications for individuals, regardless of whether they attended a prestigious university or whether they started rich or poor. Behind every student lies an individual, and behind every prominent individual lies a committed student who is dedicated to learning and getting better.

Rather than seeing individuals as defined by poverty, illiteracy, and lack of opportunity, we need to understand that education segregates empowered individuals from laypeople; it defines the prepared ones from daydreamers and achievers from nonachievers. This is evidenced across the globe, where prominence is ascribed and dedicated to education and elevating education to a pedestal. Prominent individuals who have demonstrated great knowledge range from politicians and comedians to actors and actresses. They are ordinary people who were once students like us and took matters into their own hands, performing extraordinarily due to their pledges to themselves, others, and the world at large. In fact, it would not be unfair to say that their primary endeavour was to make exceptional changes in the world they were destined to live in and conquer. Some of them include the following.

- ✓ Former US president Barack Obama
- ✓ Former UK prime minister David Cameron
- ✓ Former Taiwanese president Ma Ying-jeou
- ✓ Russian president Vladimir Putin
- ✓ Israeli prime minister Benjamin Netanyahu
- ✓ Ethiopian prime minister Hailemariam Desalegn
- ✓ Former Zimbabwean president Robert Mugabe
- ✓ Legendary actor and former California governor Arnold Schwarzenegger
- ✓ Actress Jodie Foster
- ✓ Comedian Rowan Atkinson (Mr. Bean)
- ✓ *American Idol* winner Carrie Underwood
- ✓ Actress Natalie Portman
- ✓ Successful director Spike Lee
- ✓ Actress, humanitarian, and political activist Ashley Judd

Understand the need for becoming a better student.

The progressive step of understanding the need to become a better student turns you into a student who strives for success in all areas of your life. During my undergraduate life, I thought I was going through a pedantic system of going to classes, taking notes, completing assignments with minimal interest and effort, doing revisions only a week before my due dates, barely meeting deadlines, and undergoing a lot of stress following exams, year in and year out.

During my postgraduate studies, I had this strong urge to become a better student and soon inculcated myself with an attitude to learn more, know more, and become more. I wanted to become more efficient, competitive, and consistent in my quest to make a meaningful contribution in my academic matters. In my classroom, I sat with students with competitive intelligences because I knew I had to fit in somehow. I wanted to contribute meaningfully and purposefully with them. I had to develop an effective strategy to become a student who engaged in classroom topics and contributed intelligently by making relevant points. I also ensured that I never missed out on an opportunity to learn a new concept.

Set visual academic goals.

Setting goals is a rather old cliché that a vast majority of students, looking to improve their academic results, have verbally overused but practically underused. As an undergraduate student, I never saw the merit in setting goals, let alone in writing them down. I had only two desires: (1) finish the course and (2) get better grades. However, desire alone can only make us work hard towards achieving our goal of *somehow* getting good grades. It caps the extent to which we can go intellectually and limits us in achieving our full academic potential. Exceeding expectations is a different conquest altogether. It requires a clear, smart objective that we can visually track and follow up on. As a postgraduate student, I have realised its great benefits.

Normally, businesses set SMART goals that are specific so they have a platform to work on and something to measure their end result with in order to understand their limits and outline areas of improvement. Astonishingly, you can also replicate this practice academically by setting an academic goal and measuring any progress made against it. Goal setting signifies a preparation and an attitude towards achieving excellence using a structured and organised platform. You can set a goal for short- or long-term purposes; the quality, quantity, duration, and depth are completely up to you. You take charge of your life and plan your progress towards success.

You should set your goals with a healthy blend of purpose and intelligence. They are essentially a well-defined road map of where you want to go. Goals help you maintain your focus, reduce diversions, and do things consistently for a definite period of time. They give you something to wake up for, something to wake up to, and something to be happy and proud of. You should revisit, revise, analyse, and adjust your goals, when needed; they are yours, and you belong to them. This diary is meant to organise your academic progress. It ensures you work optimally and efficiently to attain your peak academic performance. It helps you get creative with ideas; keep track of deadlines; and remember what you need to remember, like why your goal matters to you, the people who keep you going, your career goals, and so on.

Understand the benefits of academic investment.

I never fully appreciated the implication of investing in materials that would bolster my academic performance until I reached my master's level. Investing in itself is a habit that can transform your future. Upon realising its variegated benefits, I knew I needed to invest in books specific to my studies, as well as gadgets such as a recorder, a laptop, and, of course, a journal. To say the least, the end result was astonishing and rewarding—all at once. My grades went up, my interest picked up seamlessly, my motivation was restored, and I began to take on each day with a can-do attitude, settling for nothing less than that. I needed to develop an organised regimen to facilitate my desire to grow and improve my academic performance.

I started by finding out what I was worst at in class; I realised my number-one academic enemy was statistics. I just couldn't wrap my brain around it, no matter how it was taught in the class. However, I had to get the right grade for me to progress any further, so I did something called *options investment*. It basically means finding a number of explanatory materials dedicated to a specific topic. To overcome my weakness in statistics, I decided to get three different books on the same subject (statistics). They each had a different font, a different layout, a different explanation style, and a different understandable set of questions and answers. I read all three of them, focused on one that really felt like it was clicking with my brain, and then utilised it daily till it all sunk in. How well I did amazed me; I was among the top three or four students in the class in some of the phase test. I was blown away!

Know that practice shrinks the knowledge gap.

Students have an endless capacity to learn and store more; with this in mind, it turns out that we have a vacancy in our information storage and can integrate more information. This depends on how we structure what we choose to intake and how much practice we are willing to put in to obtain the information that we want to store. For me, studying is equivalent to planting seeds.

Filling the void in our knowledge requires a constant search; otherwise, we wouldn't study in the first place. Becoming a better student is just as pattern-dependent as becoming a specialist in any given field. It entails way more than merely attending classes and getting by in exams, year in and year out. The essence of education demands continuous improvement in that you need to become more to achieve more. In order to attain our academic potential, we all need to invest more time, energy, focus, and commitment into conceptualising, applying, and following through with a regimen that works best for us.

As a student, I wish I knew then what I know now. Things I know now would have enabled me to work that much smarter and harder. Being a student is a lifelong journey that takes commitment, dedication, focus, attention, development, understanding, practice, organisation, preparation, deconstruction of information, and discipline.

Acknowledge your potential to improve.

Many students just don't believe that they have what it takes to compete among the top students and to reach their desired grades. The key is to start thinking differently about your capacity to learn. You can do this by understanding your competence and areas for improvement, jotting them down in your journal, and learning from people who have been where you are and have eclipsed the worries that plague you. In addition, make it a point to feed your brain with motivational content. For example, I have found it helpful to watch motivational videos before my classes or before heading out for lectures. It tunes me up for success and helps me remember that I have what it takes to make it through.

Dedicate your full attention during class.

We all have pending messages to attend to, or interesting pieces of gossip that instantly attract our attention, or a rib-tickling joke that we need to crack right there with our classmates in the classroom. However, as students, we must know that there is a time and place for everything. Recreation, jokes, plain talk, and any other form of entertainment can wait when we are in class. We must insulate ourselves from all distractions whilst listening to the teacher. At the very least, we should respect the fact that teachers are paid to pass on relevant information to us. It is part of what they do, and they dutifully and competently share that information with us. We must respect their efforts towards our goals.

I normally turn off my phone before class or use it as a recorder; or else, I bring in a small recorder. Obviously, I need teacher permission at times to record my classes; however, I put it in my front shirt pocket, just in case.

Develop the habit of reading anything and everything you can; just read!

I have fuelled my motivation to do well academically by reading copious amounts of books that have enhanced my reading speed, vocabulary, and competence in learning. Books have also helped me highlight and pick out only relevant materials that I need. Following through with this process has really helped me; it has made my brain somehow register and understand what I am looking for, although it did take practice. I couldn't have become the better student I am today without the intense passion I developed through reading. Therefore, reading is the best practicing tool any student can afford; we have things all around us to read—no excuses. However, to improve your effectiveness, try reading materials that interest you; it keeps you wanting to read more and more!

Research resources that can help you.

In the 21st century, the means of learning and knowledge acquisition has catapulted to the point where teaching methods have assumed new shapes and forms in an attempt to accommodate individual students' academic concerns and progress. With more commitment and constant diligent from academic institutions, resources is now conveniently at our disposal. Access to learning materials has now become ever so fluid, flexible, and attainable; we can actually customise a variety of resources to our individual learning needs through social media, blogs, student forums, YouTube videos, and even mobile apps. These systems and resources have been put in place for all level of students, no matter their current stage of progress.

Previously, I never appreciated the benefits of some of these resources, nor did I seek ways to utilise them to meet my academic needs. For example, I used to not like to sit in a library or seek extra materials to study; however, I changed those attitudes the moment I knew it had come time to up the ante. We should take advantage of the library, review session, and tutor resources available to us, which can help us manage our academic competence in a way that can only improve us.

Designate time to study.

This is my favourite one; not many people can sit down and study for hours, and I am one of them! However, I realise that I don't have to study for hours at a stretch. Besides, the brain cannot healthily engage in such a lengthy chore without feeling fatigued. But I study when I study! This simply means that I have a scheduled study time each week when I sit down, turn my phone off, put the books on, and study for a maximum of three hours with breaks, without fail. I do this practice three days a week. On the first day, I read and outline key sentences or words. On day two, I take relevant notes, and I revise on day three. This narrows the information down in an accessible, relevant, and easy way.

While studying is an inevitable part of the journey of becoming a better student, how we study is a crucial part of the studying process. Previously, I repeatedly read a whole textbook; however, when I did that, I remembered less of what I had read at the end, meaning that I lost some or most of the relevant key facts I spent time revising for. Consequently, I had to follow the sam tedious process over and over again prior to my exam. I realised that, along side the process of studying, how we study what we study efficiency, determines the quality in outcome of what we aim to achieve.

Be ahead, and stay ahead.

When it comes to assignments, I detest the stress that only comes when we are approaching a deadline and we have little understanding of the assignment's subject. In other words, stress strikes us most when we are underprepared. This is where time management and organisation become so important. While I do understand that these skills take time and practice, it is vital that you learn them in order to go above and beyond. My advice to you is to start with the basics. Don't leave an assignment or any task till the eleventh hour; always strive for an early finish, which you can achieve by allocating some time to complete the task.

Seek out the most difficult subjects, and tackle them first.

Academically competent students always seek new challenges to surmount and harder problems to solve. They time their essay writing, remember key facts on the go, associate the facts with other items, and know how to access those pieces of information whenever they need them. Appreciating the need for constant challenges is just what you need to keep you hungry for more and to make you want to become more.

Do some form of exercise.

For me, exercise for the benefit of academic performance is not about getting big and strong. Our books are not so heavy that we need to spend hours bulking up in the gym. Besides, most of our study materials have become electronic, and many of us have tablets and laptops instead of stacks of books. However, doing some subtle exercises does help improve cognitive function, memory, and alertness, along with the benefit of toning muscles.

Sleep well.

It is bad enough when late-night stints or insufficient rest cause you to look gloomy or drift off in class. But what is worse is that while your eyes helplessly close, your academic performance slips. Signs of sleepiness have been suggested to adversely affect students' behaviour and emotions, as sleepiness causes them to experience problems with hyperactivity, attention, or concentration. In addition, when students are sleepy, they can miss out on relevant information shared in the classroom. Sleep, therefore, is paramount to becoming a better student and developing a better relationship with your learning materials. Sleep facilitates memory consolidation, which is essential for learning new information. It solidifies information so it stays in your memory and you can retrieve it on demand.

Researchers of animal and human studies suggest that a good sleeping habit goes a long way in enhancing academic performance, energy, focus, concentration, retention of information, and creative problem-solving skills. On the other hand, lack of sleep impairs the ability to store new information. While information acquisition and recall occur during waking hours, the consolidation of such information takes place during our rest when the neural connections that form our memories strengthen, resulting in learning outcomes such as better grades, along with the ability to focus efficiently in the classroom.

My Student Pledge Journal

JANUARY QUOTE

GEEK COMMUNITY
LEARNING THROUGH STUDENTS

"You can't connect the dots looking forward; you can only connect them looking backwards. So you have to trust that the dots will somehow connect in your future. You have to trust in something—your gut, destiny, life, karma, whatever. This approach has never let me down, and it has made all the difference in my life."
—Steve Jobs

_____

_____

_____

_____

_____

_____

_____

Personal Reflection:

GEEK COMMUNITY
LEARNING THROUGH STUDENTS

_____

_____

_____

_____

_____

_____

_____

_____

_____

_____

_____

_____

_____

_____

_____

_____

I pledge to reach my full academic potential this year.

_____

_____

_____

_____

_____

_____

_____

_____

_____

_____

_____

_____

_____

_____

_____

_____

_____

_____

_____

_____

_____

_____

_____

_____

_____

_____

_____

_____

_____

_____

_____

_____

_____

_____

_____

_____

_____

_____

I pledge to reach my full academic potential this year.

Memory Zone

#	Dates	Name (Researcher/Author)	Key Facts /Concepts to Remember
1			
2			
3			
4			

My Understanding?

My Student Pledge Journal

FEBRUARY QUOTE

GEEK COMMUNITY
LEARNING THROUGH STUDENTS

"*Everyone* here has the sense that right now is one of those moments when we are influencing the *future.*"
—Steve Jobs

_____

_____

_____

_____

_____

_____

I pledge to reach my full academic potential this year.

Personal Reflection:

_____

_____

_____

_____

_____

_____

_____

_____

_____

_____

_____

_____

_____

_____

_____

_____

_____

_____

I pledge to reach my full academic potential this year.

_____

_____

_____

_____

_____

_____

_____

_____

_____

_____

_____

_____

_____

_____

_____

_____

_____

_____

Memory Zone

#	Dates	Name (Researcher/Author)	Key Facts /Concepts to Remember
1			
2			
3			
4			

My Understanding?

I pledge to reach my full academic potential this year.

My Student Pledge Journal

MARCH QUOTE

GEEK COMMUNITY
LEARNING THROUGH STUDENTS

"The measure of who we are is what we do with what we have."

—Vince Lombardi

_____

_____

_____

_____

_____

_____

_____

Personal Reflection:

GEEK COMMUNITY
LEARNING THROUGH STUDENTS

_____

_____

_____

_____

_____

_____

_____

_____

_____

_____

_____

_____

_____

_____

_____

_____

I pledge to reach my full academic potential this year.

_____

_____

_____

_____

_____

_____

_____

_____

_____

_____

_____

_____

_____

_____

_____

_____

_____

_____

_____

_____

_____

_____

_____

_____

_____

_____

_____

_____

_____

_____

_____

_____

_____

_____

_____

_____

I pledge to reach my full academic potential this year.

Memory Zone

#	Dates	Name (Researcher/Author)	Key Facts /Concepts to Remember
1			
2			
3			
4			

My Understanding?

My Student Pledge Journal

APRIL QUOTE

GEEK COMMUNITY
LEARNING THROUGH STUDENTS

"*Start* by doing what's necessary; then do what's possible; and suddenly you are doing the *impossible.*"

—Francis of Assisi

_____

_____

_____

_____

_____

_____

I pledge to reach my full academic potential this year.

Personal Reflection:

GEEK COMMUNITY
LEARNING THROUGH STUDENTS

_____

_____

_____

_____

_____

_____

_____

_____

_____

_____

_____

_____

_____

_____

_____

_____

_____

_____

_____

_____

_____

_____

_____

_____

_____

_____

_____

_____

_____

_____

_____

_____

_____

_____

I pledge to reach my full academic potential this year.

_____

_____

_____

_____

_____

_____

_____

_____

_____

_____

_____

_____

_____

_____

_____

_____

_____

_____

Memory Zone

#	Dates	Name (Researcher/Author)	Key Facts /Concepts to Remember
1			
2			
3			
4			

My Understanding?

I pledge to reach my full academic potential this year.

My Student Pledge Journal

MAY QUOTE

GEEK COMMUNITY
LEARNING THROUGH STUDENTS

"The best preparation for tomorrow
is doing your best today."
—H. Jackson Brown Jr.

_____
_____
_____
_____
_____
_____

Personal Reflection:

I pledge to reach my full academic potential this year.

_____

_____

_____

_____

_____

_____

_____

_____

_____

_____

_____

_____

_____

_____

_____

_____

_____

_____

_____

_____

_____

_____

_____

_____

_____

_____

_____

_____

_____

_____

_____

_____

_____

_____

_____

_____

_____

_____

_____

I pledge to reach my full academic potential this year.

_____

_____

_____

_____

_____

_____

_____

_____

_____

_____

_____

_____

_____

_____

_____

_____

_____

_____

Memory Zone

#	Dates	Name (Researcher/Author)	Key Facts /Concepts to Remember
1			
2			
3			
4			

My Understanding?

I pledge to reach my full academic potential this year.

My Student Pledge Journal

JUNE QUOTE

GEEK COMMUNITY
LEARNING THROUGH STUDENTS

"*Life* is 10 percent what happens to you and 90 percent how you react to *it.*"

—Charles R. Swindoll

_____

_____

_____

_____

_____

_____

_____

Personal Reflection:

GEEK COMMUNITY
LEARNING THROUGH STUDENTS

_____

_____

_____

_____

_____

_____

_____

_____

_____

_____

_____

_____

_____

_____

_____

_____

_____

I pledge to reach my full academic potential this year.

_____

_____

_____

_____

_____

_____

_____

_____

_____

_____

_____

_____

_____

_____

_____

_____

_____

_____

_____

_____

_____

_____

_____

_____

_____

_____

_____

_____

_____

_____

_____

_____

_____

_____

_____

_____

_____

I pledge to reach my full academic potential this year.

Memory Zone

#	Dates	Name (Researcher/Author)	Key Facts /Concepts to Remember
1			
2			
3			
4			

My Understanding?

JULY QUOTE

GEEK COMMUNITY
LEARNING THROUGH STUDENTS

"Good, better, best. Never let it rest. 'Til your good is better and your better is best."

—St. Jerome

_____
_____
_____
_____
_____
_____
_____

Personal Reflection:

GEEK COMMUNITY
LEARNING THROUGH STUDENTS

_____

_____

_____

_____

_____

_____

_____

_____

_____

_____

_____

_____

_____

_____

_____

_____

_____

_____

_____

_____

_____

_____

_____

_____

_____

_____

_____

_____

_____

_____

_____

_____

_____

I pledge to reach my full academic potential this year.

_____

_____

_____

_____

_____

_____

_____

_____

_____

_____

_____

_____

_____

_____

_____

_____

_____

Memory Zone

#	Dates	Name (Researcher/Author)	Key Facts /Concepts to Remember
1			
2			
3			
4			

My Understanding?

I pledge to reach my full academic potential this year.

My Student Pledge Journal

AUGUST QUOTE

"It always seems impossible until it's done."

—Nelson Mandela

_____

_____

_____

_____

_____

_____

_____

Personal Reflection:

GEEK COMMUNITY
LEARNING THROUGH STUDENTS

_____

_____

_____

_____

_____

_____

_____

_____

_____

_____

_____

_____

_____

_____

_____

_____

I pledge to reach my full academic potential this year.

_____

_____

_____

_____

_____

_____

_____

_____

_____

_____

_____

_____

_____

_____

_____

_____

_____

_____

_____

_____

_____

_____

_____

_____

_____

_____

_____

_____

_____

_____

_____

_____

_____

_____

_____

_____

_____

I pledge to reach my full academic potential this year.

Memory Zone

#	Dates	Name (Researcher/Author)	Key Facts /Concepts to Remember
1			
2			
3			
4			

My Understanding?

My Student Pledge Journal

SEPTEMBER QUOTE

GEEK COMMUNITY
LEARNING THROUGH STUDENTS

"It does not matter how slowly you go as long as you do not stop."

—Confucius

_____

_____

_____

_____

_____

_____

_____

Personal Reflection:

GEEK COMMUNITY
LEARNING THROUGH STUDENTS

_____

_____

_____

_____

_____

_____

_____

_____

_____

_____

_____

_____

_____

_____

_____

_____

_____

_____

_____

_____

_____

_____

_____

_____

_____

_____

_____

_____

_____

_____

_____

_____

_____

_____

I pledge to reach my full academic potential this year.

_____

_____

_____

_____

_____

_____

_____

_____

_____

_____

_____

_____

_____

_____

_____

_____

_____

_____

Memory Zone

#	Dates	Name (Researcher/Author)	Key Facts /Concepts to Remember
1			
2			
3			
4			

My Understanding?

I pledge to reach my full academic potential this year.

My Student Pledge Journal

OCTOBER QUOTE

GEEK COMMUNITY
LEARNING THROUGH STUDENTS

"*Failure* is where you put it; rather than at the end, put it at the beginning, and if you keep failing, it only means you are still at the beginning of your progress. No successful person has had a successful life without a failed *beginning*."

—Samson Y. A.

_____

_____

_____

_____

_____

_____

Personal Reflection:

GEEK COMMUNITY
LEARNING THROUGH STUDENTS

_____

_____

_____

_____

_____

_____

_____

_____

_____

_____

_____

_____

_____

_____

_____

_____

I pledge to reach my full academic potential this year.

_____

_____

_____

_____

_____

_____

_____

_____

_____

_____

_____

_____

_____

_____

_____

_____

_____

_____

I pledge to reach my full academic potential this year.

Memory Zone

#	Dates	Name (Researcher/Author)	Key Facts /Concepts to Remember
1			
2			
3			
4			

My Understanding?

My Student Pledge Journal

NOVEMBER QUOTE

GEEK COMMUNITY
LEARNING THROUGH STUDENTS

"Failure will never overtake me if my determination to succeed is strong enough."

—Og Mandino

_____

_____

_____

_____

_____

_____

_____

I pledge to reach my full academic potential this year.

Personal Reflection:

GEEK COMMUNITY
LEARNING THROUGH STUDENTS

_____

_____

_____

_____

_____

_____

_____

_____

_____

_____

_____

_____

_____

_____

_____

_____

I pledge to reach my full academic potential this year.

_____

_____

_____

_____

_____

_____

_____

_____

_____

_____

_____

_____

_____

_____

_____

_____

_____

_____

_____

_____

I pledge to reach my full academic potential this year.   55

Memory Zone

#	Dates	Name (Researcher/Author)	Key Facts /Concepts to Remember
1			
2			
3			
4			

My Understanding?

I pledge to reach my full academic potential this year.

My Student Pledge Journal

DECEMBER QUOTE

GEEK COMMUNITY
LEARNING THROUGH STUDENTS

"The secret of getting ahead is getting started."

—Mark Twain

_____

_____

_____

_____

_____

_____

Personal Reflection:

GEEK COMMUNITY
LEARNING THROUGH STUDENTS

_____

_____

_____

_____

_____

_____

_____

_____

_____

_____

_____

_____

_____

_____

I pledge to reach my full academic potential this year.

_____

_____

_____

_____

_____

_____

_____

_____

_____

_____

_____

_____

_____

_____

_____

_____

_____

_____

_____

I pledge to reach my full academic potential this year.

_____

_____

_____

_____

_____

_____

_____

_____

_____

_____

_____

_____

_____

_____

_____

_____

_____

_____

_____

_____

I pledge to reach my full academic potential this year.

Memory Zone

#	Dates	Name (Researcher/Author)	Key Facts /Concepts to Remember
1			
2			
3			
4			

My Understanding?

My Student Pledge Journal

GOOD LUCK!

I pledge to reach my full academic potential this year.

My Student Pledge Journal

REFERENCES

GEEK COMMUNITY
LEARNING THROUGH STUDENTS

Quotes throughout the book were obtained from Brainy Quote (https://www.brainyquote.com).

- January (Steve Jobs):
  https://www.brainyquote.com/quotes/steve_jobs_416875
- February (Steve Jobs):
  https://www.brainyquote.com/quotes/steve_jobs_416894
- March (Vince Lombardi):
  https://www.brainyquote.com/quotes/vince_lombardi_382625
- April (Francis of Assisi):
  https://www.brainyquote.com/quotes/francis_of_assisi_121023
- May (H. Jackson Brown Jr.):
  https://www.brainyquote.com/quotes/h_jackson_brown_jr_382774
- June (Charles R. Swindoll):
  https://www.brainyquote.com/quotes/charles_r_swindoll_388332
- July (St. Jerome):
  https://www.brainyquote.com/quotes/st_jerome_389605
- August (Nelson Mandela):
  https://www.brainyquote.com/quotes/nelson_mandela_378967
- September (Confucius):
  https://www.brainyquote.com/quotes/confucius_140908l
- October (Samson Y. A.)
- November (Og Mandino):
  https://www.brainyquote.com/quotes/og_mandino_157864
- December (Mark Twain):
  https://www.brainyquote.com/quotes/mark_twain_118964

Lightning Source UK Ltd.
Milton Keynes UK
UKRC01n2148160418
321159UK00005B/37